Born with a silver spoon ... 'Don de son Parain' ('Gift from his godfather'): a French inscription on an English silver teaspoon by Peter, Anne and William Bateman, 1804.

Spoons
1650–2000

Simon Moore

D0242702

A Shire book

Published in 2005 by Shire Publications Ltd, Cromwell House,
Church Street, Princes Risborough, Buckinghamshire HP27 9AA,
UK. Website: www.shirebooks.co.uk
Copyright © 1987 and 2005 by Simon Moore. First published as
'Spoons 1650-1930' in 1987; reprinted 1990, 1993, 1996, 1999
and 2001. Second edition, with revised and extended text and
colour illustrations, 2005.
Shire Album 211. ISBN-10: 0 7478 0640 3;
ISBN-13: 978 0 7478 0640 3.
All rights reserved. No part of this publication may be reproduced
or transmitted in any form or by any means, electronic or
mechanical, including photocopy, recording, or any information
storage and retrieval system, without permission in writing from
the publishers.

British Library Cataloguing in Publication Data: Moore, Simon. Spoons 1650–2000. –
2nd ed. – (Shire album; 211) 1. Spoons – England – History 2. Spoons – England –
Collectors and collecting I. Title 745.1 ISBN-10: 0 7478 0640 3; ISBN-13: 978 0 7478 0640 3.

ACKNOWLEDGEMENTS
The author offers his thanks to those who have kindly helped in providing material
for illustration: the British Museum; the Victoria and Albert Museum; Temple Newsam
House Museum, Leeds; Bill Brown; Sanda Lipton; Leslie Spatt; Charles and Josephine
Hutchinson, Andrew Morrish; Sheldon Shapiro; the late Brian Beet. He also expresses
his gratitude to Christies, Phillips and Sothebys, and especially to those whose exper-
tise, patience and advice have helped him with the text – Helen Bennell and the late
Martin Gubbins. Photographs are acknowledged as follows: Christies, pages 6 (top
left), 16, 33 (top); Hampshire County Council Museums and Archives Service, page 8
(top); Vivica Hunter, page 55 (top); Phillips, pages 6 (bottom right), 10, 12 (bottom), 16
(bottom right), 24; Sothebys, pages 9, 13; Temple Newsam House, Leeds, page 18. All
other photographs are by the author, taken by courtesy of: the British Museum, page 5;
Sanda Lipton, page 30 (bottom right); London Company of Pewterers, page 17; Vivika,
Chenil Galleries, London, page 43 (top); Victoria and Albert Museum, pages 6 (upper
centre), 12 (upper), 20, 21 (left), 49 (lower). All other plates are by courtesy of private
collectors.

THE
BRITISH
MUSEUM
THE PAUL HAMLYN LIBRARY

Printed in Great Britain by CIT Printing Services Ltd, Press Buildings, Merlins Bridge,
Haverfordwest, Pembrokeshire SA61 1XF.

Contents

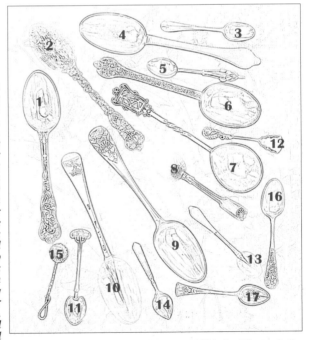

Cover: (1) Gilt bacchanalian spoon obverse, 1834; (2) vine pattern spoon reverse, 1837; (3) plain Hanoverian teaspoon, c.1760; (4) dognose tablespoon, 1704; (5) Sarepta pattern Cymric teaspoon designed by Oliver Baker or Rex Silver for Liberty, 1902; (6) gilt and engraved trefid spoon by Lawrence Coles, 1683; (7) superb Arts and Crafts spoon in Tudor style with plique á jour enamelled terminal, by either the Gaskins or the Dawsons, c.1900; (8) unusual coconut-shell bowled teaspoon, c.1800; (9) rococo tablespoon by Jeremiah Lee, 1733; (10) rat-tailed Hanoverian tablespoon with Ithell crest, by Paul Hanet, 1719; (11) tea or coffee spoon with a slender stem, swollen into a horse fetlock and with an enamelled terminal of seed pods or pomegranates, apparently designed by Ashbee and titled 'Tree of Life', for Liberty & Co, Birmingham, 1905; (12) rococo salt shovel, c.1750; (13) dognose teaspoon, c.1710; (14) Deco coffee spoon by Bernard Instone with chevron design and yellow enamel, 1937; (15) whiplash rococo salt spoon, c.1760; (16) rococo teaspoon with cherub and lyre, c.1750; (17) Art Nouveau enamel-handled teaspoon commemorating the end of the First World War, inscribed 'Peace 1919'.

Early history

Spoons have always been popular as gifts; apart from the more usual occasions such as christenings, they have been given as tokens of love and faith at weddings and as memorials at funerals. In previous centuries they were treasured since, like knives, they were an essential of ordinary life and so were carried by everyone.

Spoons have been popular as collectors' items since Victorian times; they are small, useful and often inexpensive, and their history is long and interesting. Styles varied in popularity and some were affected by historical events.

Man's first attempts at making spoons were crude by modern standards, but effective; the end of a bone or antler was scooped out or a shell was tied on to a stick. Throughout the Bronze and Iron Ages people continued to use such materials although a few spoons made from a copper alloy such as bronze have been found. Iron was impractical as a spoon-making metal.

Following the Roman invasion a large number of more sophisticated and better balanced spoons were introduced to Britain. They were made from bone, pewter, bronze and silver. The earliest examples of the spoon (*cochlear* in Latin) comprised a round bowl attached to a *stele* (narrow handle) that tapered down to a spike. The spike was used for spearing snails from their shells. Later Roman spoons show the incorporation of an elbow into the design, while the bowl became either purse-shaped or pear-shaped. By the second or third century AD another spoon design had appeared, characterised by a coiled handle and a larger bowl. It was probably used for supping

A rare example of a Roman silver folding spoon with a sliding collar to lock it open; the rabbit-head knop would have prevented the spoon from slipping into a large dish; third century AD.

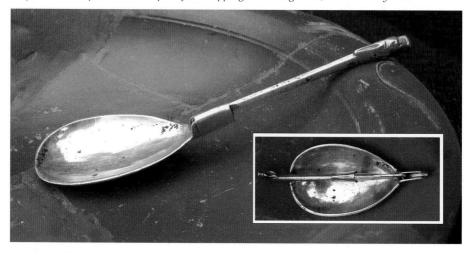

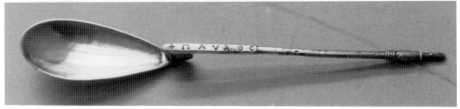

Two silver spoons of Roman form, engraved 'Saulos' and 'Paulos', from the Sutton Hoo treasure, seventh century AD.

liquids and resembles the spoons used by the Egyptians as mixing bowls for applying cosmetics rather than eating. The Romans also introduced folding cutlery that could be carried as a part of their everyday luggage. Folding spoons were made principally from copper alloy and from silver. The end of the handle was often ornamented with a silver finial or *knop*. As well as being decorative, the knop helped to prevent the spoon from sliding into a dish of food. During the fifth century Roman power in Britain crumbled but spoons still conformed to Roman design, as evidenced by those found in the Sutton Hoo ship burial.

The more outlandish culture brought by Saxon and Viking invaders soon altered the classic Roman spoon design to a broader and leaf-shaped bowl attached by a zoomorphic (animal's head) junction to a long stele. Medieval spoon bowls were rounded into a fig shape and the steles continued to be ornamented with knops; by the later fifteenth century, these were often seated on a small stepped pedestal. Spoon knops were at first either acorn-shaped or of abstract form, such as lozenge (diamond), baluster or ball, and sometimes twisted (known as *wrythen*). Later medieval spoons and those produced during the Tudor period show how the popularity of knops continued as spoon-makers adorned their wares with anthropomorphic and zoomorphic knops. The *maidenhead knop,* normally coifed with a period headdress, was the earliest of figural knops, others being the *lion sejant* or sitting lion and the *apostle*. The apostle's head was capped with a small disc (*nimbus*), which represented his halo, and he carried an identifying emblem that was often the instrument of his martyrdom.

Spoons were given as christening gifts because, like other eating implements, they were not supplied at table and therefore everyone carried their own. Social status was reflected in the type of spoon carried. Apostle spoons were especially

(Left to right) A silver maidenhead-knop spoon by John Eydes of Exeter, c.1580. Lion sejant spoon, c.1530, and the lion enlarged. An apostle knop of St Simon Zelotes, 1578.

(Left to right) A broken-off silver lion sejant knop, still with traces of gilding, c.1540, found in Romney Marsh. Unused spoon knop cast as a warrior holding a shield bearing the arms of the Painter-Stainers' Company, perhaps dropped by Francis Jackson (the maker of some such spoon sets c.1560), as it was excavated from the river Thames. It has been carved with a V-point for receiving into a V-notch at the end of the spoon handle like the seal-top knop shown on the right (c.1600), and which feature normally charac-terises London-made spoons. A seal-top spoon knop showing a stepped join (darker solder line arrowed) used by provincial makers (Norwich in this instance).

An assortment of medieval and sixteenth-century knopped spoons on an eighteenth-century spoon rack. The top row are pewter: (left to right) diamond point, two maidenhead spoons (the left with a fifteenth-century atours headdress), a larger diamond point, a baluster knop and an acorn knop. (Bottom row, left to right) Three acorn knops (one of latten), a silver seal-top (1592), a latten cone knop and a pewter melon knop.

popular as christening gifts, with the child's patron saint on top of the spoon's stele. Sometimes they were made in sets of thirteen, representing the twelve apostles with the addition of Christ as the thirteenth. Towards the end of the sixteenth century the baluster knop was capped with a disc similar to the apostle's nimbus. This arrangement, known as a *seal-top*, was also popular since the initials of the owner and donor could be pricked or engraved on to the disc rather than the stele. Knops for silver spoons were cast separately, attached to the stele by a soldered joint and then gilded. The assay office

*A unique set of spoons attributed to the London spoon-maker William Cawdell, assayed in 1592, and presented to Queen Elizabeth I by the then Lord Mayor of London, Sir Robert Tichborne. They are popularly known as the 'Tichborne Celebrities'. The topmost spoon depicts the queen herself (*QUENE ELIZABETH*).*

marks were struck on the back of the stele with the exception of the town mark, which was struck in the bowl.

Knopped spoons continued to be made during the first half of the seventeenth century, the apostle and seal-top being the most popular. The apostle knops, however, became cruder as the moulds for casting them began to wear out and the spoons were heavier and clumsier to use.

During this period a West Country spoonmaker, his mark attributed by Kent (1992) to Richard Chandler of Plymouth, made spoons knopped with a figure of an eastern deity, perhaps Buddha. They were marked with RC in a rectangle; others were marked with RC in a circle, which may be by the same maker, between 1630 and 1640. This should no longer be

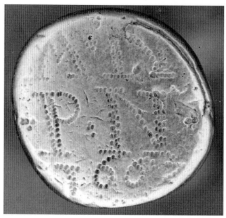

Top view of a seal-top spoon knop with pricked inscription 'AN/PN/1667'. Probably presented to a couple on the occasion of their marriage.

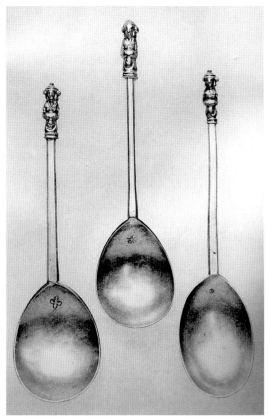

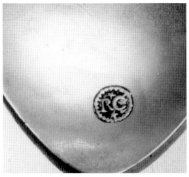

Three West Country 'Buddha-knop' spoons, c.1635 (left), and (above) a mark sometimes found on this kind of spoon, tentatively ascribed to Richard Chandler of Plymouth.

confused with the previous attribution to Raleigh Clapham of Barnstaple, who may have worked as a spoonmaker between about 1655 and 1675, when such knopped spoons were generally out of fashion.

In contrast to the more elaborately knopped spoons, the slip-top was made for people of simpler tastes, but not necessarily less well-off as many were made in silver as well as in pewter and latten (brass). The slip-top was easy to produce and could be cheap (10d per half gross for pewter in 1580). The end of the stele was cut through at an angle, leaving the handle unadorned. The slip-top spoon, already used since the later fifteenth century by those who preferred plainer pieces of silver, underwent a popular revival during Charles I's reign since its plain appearance was more appealing to puritanical taste than its more elaborate contemporaries. A pewter counterpart was produced in large numbers during the later sixteenth and early seventeenth centuries. The simpler appearance of the slip-top might account for its present comparative scarcity since many were resold for melt or, if made of pewter, were thrown away as they wore out or were broken.

Some less scrupulous goldsmiths appear to have tried

Pair of Commonwealth slip-top spoons by William Cary of London. The date letter mark for 1653 has been lifted to discourage the fraudulent addition of a knop after hallmarking.

adding a knop after the assaying of a silver slip-top spoon, to avoid paying more for the assay. The position of the date letter mark was consequently moved near the top of the stele of slip-top spoons in order to prevent such cheating, since the subsequent addition of a knop would have melted away or disfigured such a mark. This practice was continued during the Commonwealth.

A Commonwealth puritan spoon, made from latten, subsequently tinned.

Commonwealth spoons

With the ascendancy of Cromwell and Puritanism, spoons of earlier styles with religious knops fell into disfavour since they 'smacked of popery'. Some apparently had their apostle knops forcibly removed and could be distinguished from the simpler lines of the now popular slip-top spoon only by the latter spoon's thickened terminal. Not many slip-top spoons were made at this time, however, because a totally new type of spoon was produced.

With its flattened handle, completely unadorned, and its heavy elliptical bowl, the aptly named *puritan spoon* was the first spoon to show any substantial change in design for about five hundred years. Its design was probably partly contributed by immigrant Dutch and French silversmiths working in London until the outbreak of the Civil War. It was evidently popular since many were made during the Commonwealth period both in silver and in base metal. Those made from latten were subsequently tinned as the metal would otherwise taint food, especially if it had been prepared with vinegar. Spoons that were tinned were marked with the normal

A spoonmaker's mark in the bowl of a tinned latten apostle spoon, c.1670, comprising 'L R' in a circle of dots and three seal-top spoons.

Late West Country apostle spoon (St Peter), c.1660, showing a poorly cast knop due to a worn-out mould.

spoonmaker's mark of initials surrounded by the words DOUBLE WHYTED, indicating that the spoon had been twice sealed with molten tin. Many who made spoons in latten produced more adventurous punches to mark their wares. Some of the resulting touchmarks consisted of the maker's initials with one or several contemporary spoons in miniature and so clearly delineated that one can still recognise them as puritan, slip-top or seal-top.

Sometime during the Commonwealth the first post-medieval *sucket spoons* (a spoon at one end, a fork at the other) were made; the basic design resembles that of two Saxon sucket spoons found at Sevington in Wiltshire. Commonwealth sucket spoons usually show the stamp of puritan plainness. Some were made in sets of six but few seem to have survived. The forked end was used in the manner of earlier forks for eating sticky sweetmeats. Sucket spoons were not accepted as part of

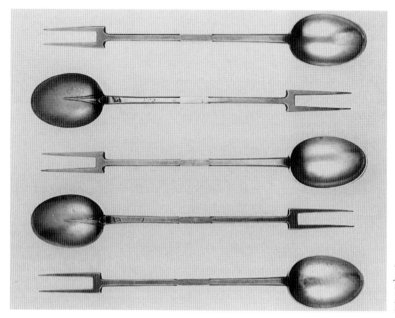

A rare set of five sucket spoons by John Smith, c.1685.

Two James I short-handled hoof spice spoons, assayed 1622 and 1612 (left and right). These appear to have been made exclusively for silver table spice boxes, which were usually ornamented with scallop-shell shaped lids. The middle spoon is a Commonwealth spice spoon of 1652.

the eventual table trio of knife, fork and spoon, which began to be used together only during the late seventeenth century.

Another sweetmeat-associated spoon was made during the Commonwealth period although its origin can be traced back to the beginning of the seventeenth century. It was designed to dip into a table spice box which stood on short silver legs and was normally shaped like a cockle shell. The spoon bowl was either oval or slightly pointed at the front. The short and wavy stele, similar to Roman 'swan-handled spoons', ended in a horse's hoof terminal. It is known as a *hoof spoon,* not to be confused with the rarer spoon from the same period with a knop shaped like a horse's hoof but with a normal straight stele and fig-shaped bowl.

Puritan spoons were sometimes filed with one, two or three notches at the top of the handle. The reason for this simple decoration is not known. It has also been noted on the handle of the earliest known English silver fork (1632), the basic design of which was copied exactly from French forks of that period, and occasionally on spoons as late as 1670. The notches may have been a precursor of the new-styled terminal that appeared during the Restoration period on spoons and later on forks.

The later seventeenth century

With the restoration of the monarchy in 1660 sacred and fancy knops came back into favour and some older styles of knopped spoons were revived. The puritan spoon design, although still popular, was quickly modified to fit in with the changing fashion brought over from France by Charles II, the *trefid spoon* evolving directly from it. Its terminal was broadened and either formed into three lobes or filed with two notches, giving the appearance of a cloven hoof, which is why it is sometimes also known as *pied de biche*. Spoonmakers also lengthened the *peg*, where the bowl meets the handle, into a tapering support known as a *rat-tail* (also found on the reverse of some Roman spoon bowls) running longitudinally underneath the bowl.

The back of the bowl and the front of the spoon handle were sometimes embossed with a swirling design known as *lacework*, which was either carved into the spoon mould or

Two pewter trefid spoons with one teaspoon and a chocolate spoon, dated 1690; to the right a pewter dognose spoon, c.1710, and a more elongated trefid teaspoon; on a beechwood trencher.

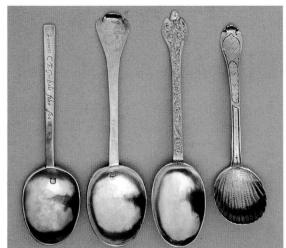

Left: *(Left to right) A Puritan spoon by Steven Venables, London, 1652, with a contemporary donation inscription. An Exeter trefid, the handle of which appears to have been beaten out and filed with trefid notches to comply with the new trend, and pricked 'I+P' over 'I+P 1676' on the reverse of the peg-jointed bowl – another sign that it may have been originally made as a Puritan spoon. A finely engraved London gilt trefid spoon by Laurence Coles, 1683. A rare York trefid spoon by Robert Williamson, 1686, converted c.1941 into a sugar ladle! The original hallmarks are still visible on the reverse of the handle and much of the other decoration may well be original.*
Below: *The reverse of these spoons.*

template or else subsequently chased on to the spoon. Other spoons were lavishly engraved all over with foliage, the rat-tail support forming the rib of an engraved acanthus leaf under the bowl. The traditional town mark was moved from the bowl to the reverse of the handle with the other assay marks, since a hard blow struck in the bowl by the assayer's punch would have dented the rat-tail.

Silver trefid spoons were made by the traditional forging method of hammering out each end of an ingot into a rough spoon shape. The centre of the bowl's reverse was left untreated, leaving a raised tapering area for forming the rat-tail. The handle was hammered along both edges to give it strength and the bowl was dished into a lead template. The spoon surface was then planished. The stele to bowl junction was hammered against a rod-shaped anvil to form an angle

*A range of trefid spoons show-
ing a variety of terminals. The
back of the bowl of the left-hand
spoon has been ornamented with
lacework.*

*The reverse of three trefid spoons show-
ing one plain and two beaded rat-tail bowl
supports. Note the engraved stars on the
middle spoon's terminal.*

Pewter dognose spoons commemorating the coronation of Queen Anne in 1702 and (right) a close-up of the middle spoon's terminal.

and the end of the handle (terminal) was turned up in a similar manner. Finally the spoon was filed to the desired shape and polished.

During the later seventeenth century spoons were sometimes cast in moulds. The molten metal was poured into the pre-heated mould, usually made from bronze, and when it had cooled slightly the spoon was removed, the sprue (waste) was cut off and the spoon was finished with a file, some even with a planishing hammer and polish. Base-metal examples were nearly always cast and the moulds were sometimes carved with ornamentation or a design to commemorate a special occasion such as the coronation of Queen Anne.

Base-metal spoons were also made by itinerant spoonmakers, whose less well-finished products can occasionally be found. Such a spoonmaker would have carried a set of letter punches so that a purchaser's initials could be hammered into the spoon. Initials were usually engraved into silver, often in a triangle, the upper letter being the surname initial.

Whereas spoons had previously been used for eating all manner of food, two smaller-sized spoons appeared during the 'trefid period' (about 1660–1710). The earliest tea and dessert spoons were made as smaller versions of the tablespoon, which previously had a universal function and which was now reserved for soup. Many tea and dessert spoons were similarly decorated with foliate engraving according to the fashion of the period.

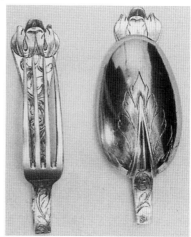

Engraved folding trefid spoon and fork,
shown extended (left) and folded (above).

Another type of spoon that was engraved in like manner was the much less common *folding spoon*, revived at this time. English examples are particularly rare. There is one medieval diamond-point spoon, found at Scarborough, which has been hinged at the base of the stele. A sliding collar shaped like a Saxon helmet can be moved over the hinged section to lock the spoon in an open position. During the trefid spoon period a few silversmiths made folding spoons and forks hinged at the bowl to stele junction. A movable collar was added which slides down the stele over a small silver tongue attached to the bowl so that the spoon (or fork) could be locked open.

After a long period of disfavour table forks began to be accepted and (about 1680) were made singly or in sets of six or twelve, as also were spoons. Together spoons and forks have

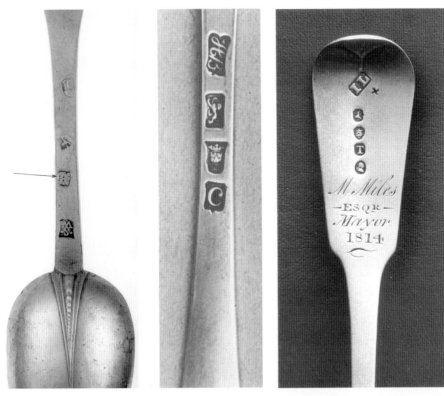

Positioning of silver hallmarks. (Left to right) Trefid spoon, 1693, showing the town mark (arrowed), now moved alongside the other hallmarks, which are more evenly spaced; later eighteenth-century spoon showing marks for 1778 close together on the reverse of the stem (bottom-marked); and a set for 1814 struck on the terminal (see pages 37 and 40).

become known as *flatware* (as opposed to *hollow ware* – beakers and other vessels for the table).

Spoonmakers all over Britain produced many more spoons than previously. In the West Country particularly, there were goldsmiths working in many towns and, rather than being sent for assay at Exeter, their spoons were marked locally and some have survived from Taunton, Truro, Barnstaple, Bristol and Plymouth. Local smiths used silver from mines around Combe Martin or in the surrounding Devon countryside.

Many West Country (and some northern) trefid spoons were characterised by a broadly splayed trefid end and others were additionally decorated with chased circles on the stele. In the north of England and in Scotland spoon handles were also chased with circles and capped with disc finials – a characteristic Scottish feature since the later sixteenth century. A few examples were engraved with a skull and sobering inscriptions such as THINK ON or LIVE TO DIE and DIE TO LIVE, showing that people were still as obsessed with mortality as their medieval ancestors. These spoons were sometimes

Left to right: *York 'memento mori' spoon by Thomas Mangy, 1670. The disc end engraved with a skull and, on the reverse of the disc, a woman's coat of arms; along the stele* LIVE TO DIE/DIE TO LIVE.

(From top) Marrow spoon by Thomas Issod, 1695, engraved with acanthus decoration; marrow spoon by William Petley, 1718; two-ended marrow scoop with beaded stele, by George Smith and William Fearn, 1788.

A child's pewter Puritan spoon, c.1660, and a variation of the slip-top, known as a stump-top spoon, c.1640.

Left: *A West Country spoon characteristically chased with circles, dated 1679.*

engraved with the name of the deceased and given as a memorial to relatives at funerals, perhaps also as gloomy reminders of their own inevitable death.

Some spoons of the trefid period and later were made with narrower handles that were scooped out along one side so that they could be used for extracting marrow from bones prepared especially for this purpose. Eventually the taste for marrow became so popular that by the mid eighteenth century two-ended scoops were being made to accompany the usual service of flatware. The fashion continued into the early nineteenth century and a few silver-plated examples were made for those with lesser means, but very few seem to have been made in base metal, presumably as those who could not afford the luxury of silver were not interested in owning a spoon made for the sole purpose of eating bone marrow.

The early eighteenth century

At the end of the seventeenth century the trefid spoon began to be displaced by a new style, the trefid notches disappearing, leaving the central part of the terminal standing alone. This wavy end is usually known as *dognose* (it faintly resembles a hound's head), although it is sometimes called *shield-top*. The dognose spoon prevailed throughout the reign of Queen Anne and is occasionally called a 'Queen Anne spoon'. The flattened trefid-style handle narrowed and became more rounded in section. The bowl was still supported with a rat-tail but was more elongated than the trefid and the spoon started to resemble the design used today. Spoonmakers preferred to make some of their spoons without dognose ends, as these were rather uncomfortable to hold, and produced just a plainly rounded terminal, which, like the trefid and dognose spoons, turned up at the end. The new-styled handle also embodied a central spine of metal running longitudinally from the terminal to the narrow shaft of the spoon. These changes in design increased in popularity so that by the time of George I's accession in 1714 the new pattern was fast becoming accepted as the standard and has been nicknamed *Hanoverian*.

An early eighteenth-century snuffbox with a rat-tailed snuff spoon fitted into its special slot under the lid.

A pair of dognose tablespoons with flattened steles in the trefid style by Edward Gibson, 1704; a teaspoon, c.1710; an earlier tiny snuff spoon by Pierre Harrache, about 1690.

Above: *Hanoverian rat-tail spoons, 1710–1725, showing the range of sizes: table, tea and snuff. The left-hand spoon has been engraved with the arms of Douglas.*

Reverse sides of Hanoverian spoons showing double-drop (left), an Irish single-drop, and two Scottish variations on the right; about 1740–60.

A group of Hanoverian pewter spoons: a tablespoon, a dessert spoon and three teaspoons, c.1750, together with a shell-back teaspoon mould on a contemporary London-made pewter plate.

Around 1715 the rat-tail was gradually superseded by a much shorter strengthening known as a *drop*, which took several different forms – the double drop and the sometimes extended single drop. The two overlapped each other for about thirty years. From this period silver flatware was acquired by industrialists eager to use and display their new-found wealth, with the result that it is easier for collectors to assemble services. Between 1730 and 1760 the bowl was made longer in relation to the handle and the handle's central spine was

Hanoverian flatware showing (from left) a spoon with a long central spine on the handle, c.1715; a long-handled provincial spoon, Dundee, c.1730; a short-handled, long-bowled London spoon, c.1750; and another c.1770.

shortened; later examples show how the balance was altered about 1770, the bowl becoming shorter and the handle longer – perhaps to conform with the Old English design (see below) which was, by then, superseding the Hanoverian. The ends of spoon and fork handles continued to turn up and crests, coats of arms or initials were engraved on the flat backs of the terminals. It had been customary since the introduction of flatware that when laying such spoons or forks on the table the concave side was laid face down so that the hallmarks (struck on the stem) and owner's markings, either on the back of the handle or on the drop, were both visible. During the 1730s some people appear to have preferred their spoons and forks to be laid the other way up. Spoon handles were therefore turned down at the ends and for the next forty years turned up or down depending on which way they were required to be laid on the table. Fork handles turned up, with rare exceptions, since a downturned fork handle is rather uncomfortable to hold. The later design of spoon with the downturned handle is called *Old English* and lacks the central spine running down the handle, which helps to distinguish it from its close relative, the Hanoverian.

Teaspoons became commonplace during the mid eighteenth century since the taking of tea had become both a novelty and a luxury. The lines of the teaspoon, like its trefid forebear, followed those of the larger tablespoons. The exuberance of

Set for tea, c.1750– 60, with a large sugar loaf and a pair of sugar nips (not sturdy enough to cut the loaf – this would have been done with a kitchen- based sugar-loaf cutter with steel blades), a tea bowl, a teapoy (for storing the dry leaves) and a teacup, with contemporary teaspoons, and including a slightly later coconut-shell bowled spoon with silver handle and a mote spoon for picking out stray tea-leaves from the cups.

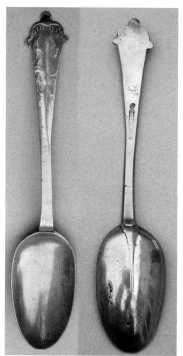

A rather worn George III pewter tablespoon, c.1761, made to commemorate his marriage to Queen Charlotte, whose initials appear next to his at the top. Later spoons were less polite and lampooned the king as 'Farmer George'.

the rococo period also affected the humble teaspoon and, to a lesser extent, other table flatware. The undersides of spoon bowls were sometimes stamped with small shells, and scrolls and rocaille work were sometimes similarly applied to the fronts of the handles with an occasional amorino or mask. By the time of George III's accession in 1760 the scrolls and shells had been superseded by more adventurous designs. A fairly common motif found on the back of a teaspoon bowl was a galleon in full sail or a bird sitting on top of its cage with the motto above its head I LOVE LIBERTY, referring to John Wilkes and his views on freedom of speech (1768). Less common designs for *picture-back* teaspoons may still be found today, and some previously unknown 'pictures' have been produced by imaginative fakers.

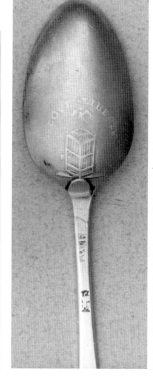

Far left: *Three cast fancy-front rococo teaspoons, c.1750.*
Left: *Bowl and stem of a picture-back teaspoon depicting a domestic bird sitting on its cage with the words I LOVE LIBERTY, referring to John Wilkes and liberty; c.1770, by Thomas Wallis.*

A scallop-bowled teaspoon with feather edging, c.1770, with a contemporary famille rose chocolate cup.

An added refinement for tea drinking was the *mote skimmer* or *mote spoon*. A hostess may have used this spoon either to remove floating tea-leaves from her guests' cups before she passed them round or for spooning the tea from the caddy into the pot. Tea then contained much dust, which was filtered from the tea-leaves through the pierced bowl. The piercing of the mote-spoon bowl was at first confined to simple holes but became more elaborate during the rococo period as silversmiths became more adventurous with decoration and showed their skills with saw and file. The spiked end of the mote spoon's stele bears a similarity to the Roman *cochlear* and balances with the delicate bowl. Some authors have suggested that it was used for dislodging tea-leaves from the grille of the teapot spout. Its actual use is still uncertain as

A set of six varied picture-back teaspoons in a contemporary case, c.1750, with a mote spoon, a pair of sugar nips and a slightly later, unusual coconut-shell bowled teaspoon with a silver handle (unmarked).

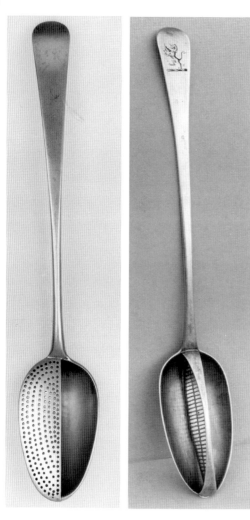

Two later eighteenth-century spoons show-ing different styles of strainer: (far left) by Hester Bateman, 1775, and (near left) by George Smith and William Eley, 1793.

other, much larger *strainer spoons* of similar appearance, complete with spiked finial, were made at this time.

The history of strainer spoons can be traced back to the Roman period, but few were made from silver in England until the mid seventeenth century. The first English type was made by drilling holes in the bowl of a contemporary tablespoon. The spoon was then re-weighed and the silversmith scratched its new weight on to the reverse side of the bowl. Eighteenth-century strainer spoons were made as optional extras to a table service and were largely used for straining lumps out of gravy. Either the spoon bowl was half-covered by a pierced grille soldered along one side of the bowl or a bridge, pierced and filed with narrow slots, was soldered longitudinally down the centre of the bowl. The bridges of

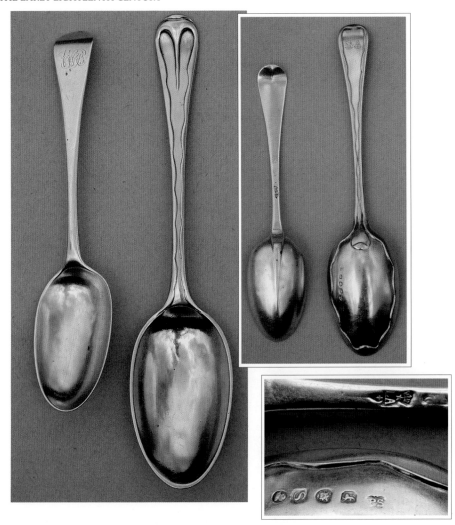

Two spoons by two of England's leading goldsmiths of their time. The rather superior Hanoverian gilt tablespoon (right) was from Paul Storr's workshop and assayed in 1813, copied from patterns from the 1720s; the wavy borders are more characteristic of spoons by Paul de Lamerie, who made the very plain Old English dessert spoon alongside. The Lamerie spoon was sold at auction for twice as much as one of the Storr spoons, showing how people will collect just for the mark!

later examples were removable for easier cleaning.

Another spoon associated with tea drinking evolved during the later eighteenth century. As tea was then a precious commodity, it was locked away from the servants in a silver or wooden caddy. In order to serve it more decorously, rather than just using an ordinary spoon, tea was put into the teapot with a *caddy spoon*. The mote spoon became outmoded; perhaps

An exceptionally fine example of a simulated filigree tea-caddy spoon centred by two doves holding an olive branch and flanked (left) by the Prince of Wales's plumes and (right) the royal crown ; by Cocks & Bettridge (mark above), c.1820.

Two cast silver-gilt caddy spoons in the form of vine leaves, by George Unite, Birmingham, 1850.

Two teaspoons to beware. The upper one is Hanoverian, c.1750, with later (Victorian) decoration; the lower spoon (c.1720) has been broken and crudely repaired (see the solder line across the bowl) – it was beaten out and the edge was trimmed where it was too thin after the reshaping!

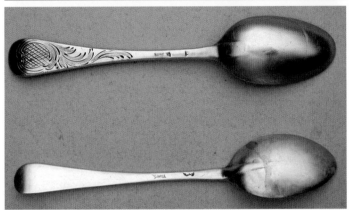

The reverse of the teaspoons shown above.

its small bowl, which was less practical for spooning tea into the pot, and the introduction of a strainer attached to the end of the teapot spout solved the problem of floating tea-leaves. Caddy spoons first appeared during the 1760s as silver-mounted shells or short-handled versions of table flatware. By 1800 the makers had become more inventive, producing spoons shaped like a jockey's cap or an eagle's wing. Others were shaped as shovels, prettily engraved and mounted with pearl or ivory handles. A few Victorian silversmiths produced superb cast examples incorporating leaves or a fisherman holding a rayed scallop shell. Many caddy spoons were made by Birmingham silversmiths who are more usually associated with vinaigrette and snuffbox making.

Specialised types of spoon

Spoons even smaller than teaspoons had been made either as toys or for the taking of snuff since Charles II's reign. Dandies and other fastidious partakers no longer needed to dirty their hands or white gloves and some snuffboxes were made with a small slot under the lid to hold the spoon in place (page 22). Other minute spoons and other flatware were made in sets of six or a dozen for use as dolls' house toys, particularly in the Netherlands. It is often difficult to distinguish between single spoons from such sets and snuff spoons.

In contrast to the minuteness of snuff and toy spoons, considerably larger silver spoons, up to 25 inches (635 mm) long, were made for serving at table and maybe in the kitchens of the nobility. The first silver basting spoons appeared during the early years of Charles II's reign. The handles of these spoons were normally hollow, made from rolled silver sheet

(Clockwise from left) Three enamel-decorated spoons (4 cm) from Portugal, c.1950; scarce dognose snuff spoon, by Pierre Harrache, c.1690; George I rat-tail Hanoverian snuff spoon, c.1720; Old English snuff spoon with acorn drop to the back of the bowl, c.1760; Art Nouveau miniature spoon in the form of an iris, c.1900; Jensen miniature spoon, c.1930, incorporating the Bindesbøll cloud pattern.

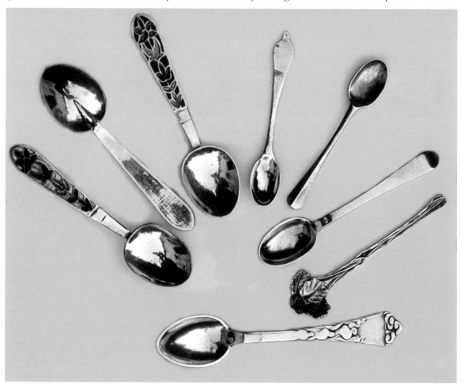

Charles II period hollow-handled basting spoon (centre), 1683, showing the underside of the bowl engraved with the arms of Burton and the initials 'F B'. A Hanoverian basting spoon (left), 1711, and a dognose baster by Henry Greene (right), 1706.

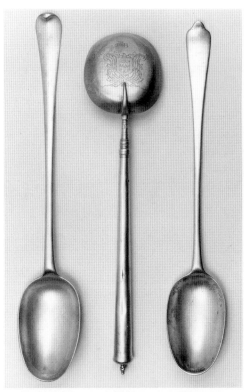

so that they would not burn the hands of their users. The large spoon bowls were frequently engraved on the underside with their owner's complete armorial bearings. Later examples show that the idea of a hollow handle, although kinder to the hands, was impractical because the silver tube would dent or split, especially if the spoon was dropped.

Below: A mixture of styles and periods, showing how well they can be combined. On the left is an Omar Ramsden and Alwyn Carr mustard pot (1910) with an Arts and Crafts mustard spoon (c.1900); on the French side plate (c.1800) is a smaller mustard spoon, c.1750; to the right is a fine salt cellar cast as a Hippopus clam shell with coral and wrack feet by Mortimer & Hunt, 1843; its shell-bowled spoon can be seen to the immediate right; below are a group of mid-eighteenth-century rococo and plain salt spoons and salt shovels with whiplash, scrolling and plain Hanoverian handles.

Fancy condiment spoon cast as a convolvulus, c.1770.

Spoons for basting or for removing stuffing (a small bowl on a long handle to reach inside a large bird and normally used at the table) were forged from one solid piece of silver like tablespoons.

The trencher salt cellars from which diners had served themselves with a pinch of salt since early medieval times were superseded during the mid eighteenth century by salt cellars from which salt was taken in a more refined manner using a spoon, rather than with the fingertips or knife points. Hanoverian salt-spoon bowls were normally shovel-shaped, attached to a short upturning handle, and were either left plain or ornamented in the same manner as teaspoons. Old English salt spoons with the more familiar round bowls became fashionable during the 1770s. The interiors of many salt-spoon bowls were gilded to protect them from the corrosive action of prolonged contact with salt. The rear of the bowl was not gilded, suggesting that the spoon was laid upside down on the salt itself or the edge of the cellar when not in use.

Mustard was served as dry powder in a 'blind' caster (without holes) from about 1700, using a long-handled and small-bowled spoon. During the 1760s mustard powder began to be moistened with water or vinegar served in a drum-shaped mustard pot. Mustard spoons are less common than salt spoons and are characterised by more elongated bowls and longer handles so that they would not fall inside the mustard pot. Subsequently both types of condiment spoon retained their basic shapes but altered in pattern according to the fashion.

The mid eighteenth century to the mid nineteenth century

A further design of spoon appeared during the mid eighteenth century, apparently taking its name from a Speaker of the House of Commons, Sir Arthur Onslow. The *Onslow pattern* was based on the standard spoon designs of the period but was enhanced by a cast scrolled knop that was attached separately by a diagonal (scarf) joint, rather in the manner of an earlier knopped spoon. The longer-handled serving pieces of Onslow flatware have a particularly pleasing balance and elegant appearance.

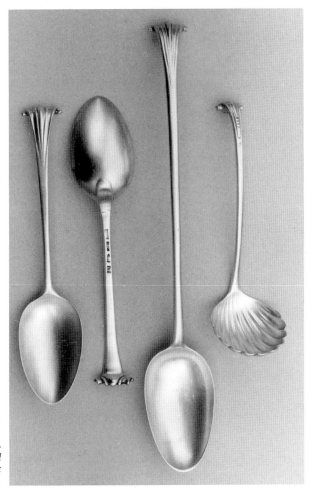

Onslow flatware: two table-spoons, a serving spoon and a shell-bowled sauce ladle; c.1766–76.

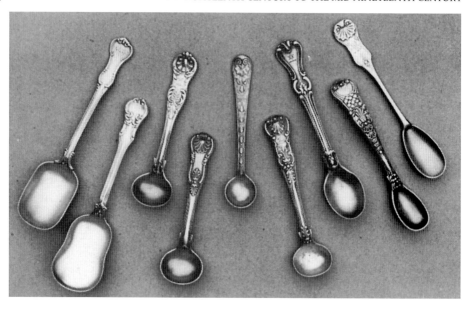

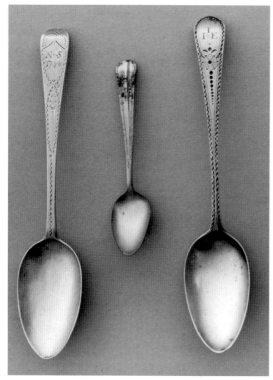

Above: *A selection of nineteenth-century patterns: (left to right) 'Princess Number 1' pattern sugar spoon, 1876; 'Victoria' pattern sugar spoon, 1842; 'Dolphin' pattern salt spoon, 1846 (the dolphins surround the shell at the top); 'King's' pattern salt spoon, 1831; 'Elizabethan' pattern salt spoon, 1890; 'Queen's' pattern salt spoon, 1852; 'Albert' pattern egg spoon, 1839; 'Coburg' pattern mustard spoon, 1840; Scottish variant of 'King's' pattern mustard spoon, Glasgow, 1827.*

Three bright-cut decorated Old English spoons, c.1770–80. The middle spoon is made from Sheffield plate, with darker areas of copper showing where the silver-plated layer has worn away.

Sheffield-plated flatware: (left) Old English table fork, c.1780; fiddle pattern tablespoon, c.1800; fiddle and thread table fork, c.1810.

Towards the end of the eighteenth century the Old English pattern completely supplanted the Hanoverian. From 1781 onwards the London assay office introduced a mechanical system of hallmarking, using a stub of four hallmarks together. Since this was easier to apply to a broader area of metal, London hallmarks were struck on the underside of the terminal. Stem-struck marks, moreover, were occasionally found to weaken the stem to the extent of forming stress cracks. Provincial assay offices followed suit during the next few years.

The discovery that silver could be fused on to copper was made by Thomas Boulsover, a Sheffield silversmith, during the mid eighteenth century. Articles with the appearance and feel of silver could be produced at a fraction of the cost, particularly pleasing for those whose social aspirations exceeded their means. Sets of early Sheffield-plated teaspoons can be found although many have lost much of their silver plating. Larger plated spoons were less common at this time (about 1760–70) and were not made in significant numbers until the second quarter of the nineteenth century. Most nineteenth-century plated flatware was made by the close-plating technique. An article was made in base metal (normally carbon steel) and tinned. It was then enveloped in a sheet of silver foil and a hot iron was passed over it so that the tin and silver fused together. Silver on copper fusion was more favoured for hollow ware and both processes were used until the discovery and harnessing of electricity led to the technique of electroplating. The electroplating process was found to be cheap, rapid and effective, and quality gave way to quantity as demands for plated wares grew. Electroplating was carried out on to nickel, and wares were marked EPNS (electroplated nickel silver).

All types of plated flatware exactly followed the designs of their silver counterparts; most were made in Sheffield, some in Birmingham. Makers' marks can be seen stamped on to the terminals of electroplated spoons in the manner of silver hallmarks, each initial occupying a separate pseudo-hallmark, such as T B & S for Thomas Bradbury & Sons or E & Co for Elkington & Company. Some platers, such as Mappin & Webb, Walker & Hall and Elkington, were particularly successful and opened salerooms in London.

An early nineteenth-century Sheffield-plated spoon tray with two modern chromium-plated apostle-style teaspoons that were popular in the 1950s, with four silver apostle-style teaspoons, which demonstrate the decorative influence of early medieval decoration, 1903; by Mappin & Webb.

Electroplaters' marks, including that of Elkington (left), c.1880–1910.

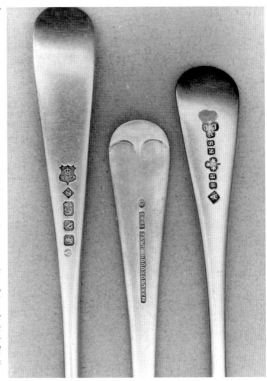

Old English pattern silver flatware handles were often enhanced (about 1770) with bright-cut engraving or feather-edging, giving an added sparkle. A simpler and not dissimilar effect could also be achieved with the die-stamping process, patented by William Darby of Sheffield in 1785. Examples bearing his WD PATENT mark are, however, rare.

From about 1790 many Scottish and northern English spoons were produced with longer and broader handle terminals as a variation of Old English pattern. They show French influence and may have been produced by Jacobites who favoured France

Below: (From top) A fine feather-edged Old English tablespoon by George Smith, 1780, inscribed to IB from BB, 'Born ye Jan. 11th 1782'. Two similar dessert spoons, also by George Smith, 1773, but note the added cartouche and engraved scrolling plant motif, known as 'Carrington shield'.

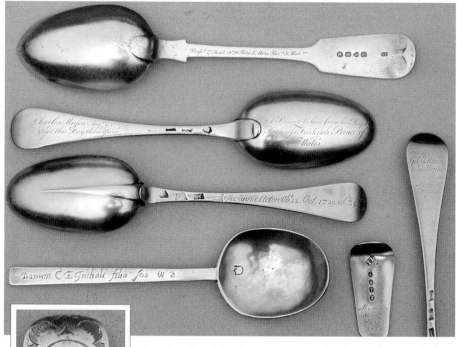

A series of mainly Georgian spoons with interesting inscriptions. (From top) Fiddle pattern spoon, assayed in 1871, with Victorian engraving, perhaps given as a forty-fifth birthday present to 'Jean Mourant Né 18 Août Bap(tis)é 27 Août, 1826 Père et Mère, Par(ai)n et Mar(ai)ne' (the inset, left, shows the obverse of the terminal). Hanoverian tablespoon, 1745, presented to 'Charles Mason, Aug(u)st y(e) 8th 1750. Aged this day 3 years. A present to him from his Royal Highness Frederick Prince of Wales'. A memento mori spoon, by Starling Wilford, 1728: 'Susanna Acton Ob(iit) 12 Oct. 1729 aet 39'. Christening Puritan spoon by Steven Venables, 1652: 'Donum C E Tintiali filio suo W B'. (Lower right-hand corner, left to right) Terminal of fiddle pattern spoon, 1814, presented to the Mayor of Leicester, inscribed 'M. Miles – Esqr - Mayor', 1814. Terminal of Hanoverian spoon by Elias Cachart, 1758, inscribed 'The Gift of Giles Pancher to his Nephew Jonathan Hewlett 1764'.

at that time. The new pattern was a precursor of the well-known fiddle pattern and is known to some as *fiddle without shoulders* but has been more conveniently nicknamed *oar*, since the broadened handle has some resemblance to an oar. Another precursor of the fiddle pattern was the *shouldered Old English*, which had been produced since the middle of the century. *Fiddle pattern* flatware began to grace southern tables sometime during the 1780s.

Scottish fiddle pattern was entirely different in style. It was made for about fifty years (*c.*1740–90) and was used almost solely for making teaspoons and some salt spoons.

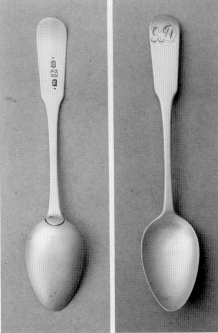

Scottish fiddle pattern teaspoon (left) by Milne and Campbell of Glasgow, c.1760. Oar pattern dessert spoon (right) by Nathaniel Gillett of Aberdeen, c.1800.

Fiddle pattern tea and dessert spoons, c.1800–20; the spoon on the right, from Newcastle, shows the Scottish influence in being longer and more slender.

It is not a variant of conventional English fiddle pattern and resembles more strongly the designs of period French and other northern spoons – the Jacobites were probably cocking a snook at the English – so the handles ended in a violin shape. Scottish fiddle pattern should not be confused with conventional fiddle, which when made in Scotland resembles the English fiddle but is longer and more slender.

The English fiddle pattern and the Old English pattern have become standard spoon designs, with many variations and decorations added during the early nineteenth century. Of these the best-known are *King's* and *Queen's* but there were also variations that sometimes combined with characteristics from other patterns. The permutations are endless. New flatware patterns continued to appear throughout the nineteenth century and most patterns were collated into a

A table knife and gilt dessert spoon by William Theobalds, 1834, using the bacchanalian pattern moulds designed and made by Thomas Stothard and Francis Chantrey, originally for Rundell, Bridge & Rundell.

book produced by the Chawner Company around 1875. One that appeared about 1880, now known as *Albany*, resembles the Onslow pattern and confusion has often arisen between the two. Albany pattern was particularly popular at the end of the nineteenth century and examples can still be found quite easily.

A modification was introduced by Victorian silversmiths when the fashion for heavily decorated wares was at its height. Many Georgian and some earlier plain spoons were 'improved' (about 1880) with scallop-edged bowls centred with a *repoussé* design of fruit, and these are known as *berry spoons*. Some spoons that underwent this treatment were decorated in a more interesting way. The practice continues today.

A vine-pattern spoon, fork and knife by William Theobalds, 1837.

'Albany' pattern teaspoons by Walker & Hall, Sheffield, 1912.

Bottom: *Examples of Victorian decoration applied to plain Georgian tablespoons from the 1760s, the Mughal style of decoration being popular at the time of the Raj. The upper dessert spoon (1789) is a more typical example, giving rise to the term 'berry spoon'. Many collectors regard this as Victorian vandalism although finely converted berry spoons often command higher prices than the original spoons!*

Below: *Detail of the Mughal-style bird in the bowl of the berry spoons at the bottom.*

An electroplated nickel silver soup spoon, c.1880, with an attachable guard for gentlemen who followed the fashion of growing a moustache.

Round-bowled *soup spoons* were not made until the end of the nineteenth century. The tablespoon, which had previously been used for this purpose, was now made slightly larger for use as a *serving spoon*. The bowl of the soup spoon is notably similar to that of round-bowled medieval spoons but the handle was made in the style of twentieth-century Old English and fiddle patterns.

LOVE SPOONS

The origins of giving a hand-made object, particularly a spoon, as a token of love, are lost in the mists of time but the term 'spooning' has long been used as a rural expression to describe a couple who were more than just friends but not necessarily lovers, although it has rather fallen out of use nowadays. The giving of such a spoon seems to have been traditional in the West of England and particularly in Wales. The earliest surviving love spoons date from the 1660s and were hand-crafted by men who would perhaps while away the long winter evenings by carving a single piece of wood into a spoon as a symbolic gift for a woman whom they were intent on wooing or just friendly with.

The type of wood used varied according to availability but most love spoons appear to have been carved from sycamore. The intricacy of the design and the skill of the carving developed through the ensuing two centuries, reflecting the depth of the maker's feelings, his patience and his dexterity. Spoons were also carved with attached chains, some with

A modern Welsh love spoon design signifying the lovers' knot expressed in Celtic interlace.

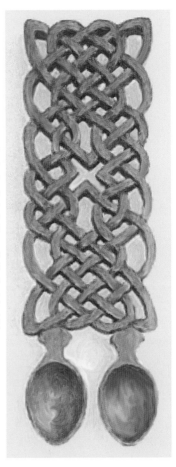

heart-shaped links or a caged rolling ball – all fashioned from a single piece of wood!

Most spoons comprise an intricately carved handle, some with sawn fretwork and hand engraving that incorporated symbolic motifs referring to the maker's future life with his lady. Some spoons are carved with words in Welsh, sometimes of a nationalistic nature, more usually expressions of tenderness, with the name of the intended recipient. Some were made with two bowls, symbolising the hoped-for future unity in marriage; a few had three or even more bowls, perhaps symbolising future children's mouths to feed, or possibly simply balancing the size of the elaborate handle.

Nowadays love spoons are made in workshops by professional carvers who produce them for sale as souvenirs or anniversary gifts, and love-spoon competitions are held as part of the Eisteddfod. Since these spoons are now purchased by the donor rather than hand-made, much of the true meaning and sentiment of traditional love spoons has rather faded.

The Arts and Crafts Movement to the present day

Table cutlery and flatware were shaped by the gradual development of a revival of previous styles, particularly medieval, later to be mixed with influences from many lands, such as the Far East. As early as the 1850s, the new styles and influences began to make their appearance in many media. By the 1870s there were innovative designers such as the renowned Dr Christopher Dresser, whose work continued to influence his successors up to sixty years later. He combined ergonomics with angularity and dispensed with fussy Victorian decoration in place of functionality and contrasting mixed materials (such as silver or electroplate with ebony). The Arts and Crafts Movement brought a rebirth of traditional styles and methods

A selection of twentieth-century English spoons. (Left to right) A pair of large soup-type spoons made for Liberty and assayed in 1899; a fine Oxford University armorial spoon by A. E. Jones, 1910, for G. Payne & Son; a typical Omar Ramsden spoon with a stem comprising flattened and twisted silver wires forming a flattened terminal of stylised seed pods; three spoons with trefoil terminals by various makers but designed by C. R. Mackintosh, the middle spoon of electroplate showing its origins in the renowned Glaswegian tearooms; a later spoon of similar form by Bernard Cuzner, 1950, who formerly worked for Liberty.

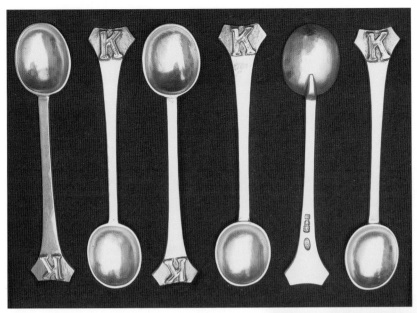

Above: *A set of small spoons by Frederick Smythe-Greenwood, London, 1913, showing that the influence of the Arts and Crafts Movement was still apparent at the time.*

Dessert spoon by Frederick Elkington, Birmingham, 1877. The engraved design combines influence from India with the Aesthetic Movement.

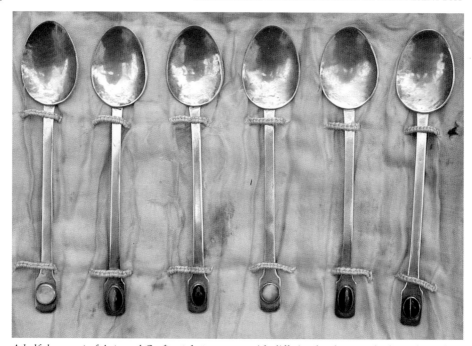

A half-dozen set of Arts and Crafts style teaspoons with differing hardstone cabochons, by Nelson Dawson, 1919, in their original silk-lined textile roll.

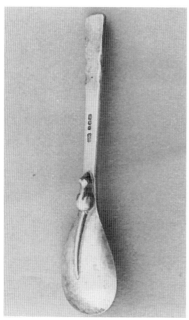

of manufacture, with its followers making many types of object by hand. Most of the craftspeople who made jewellery were also silversmiths and spoonmakers; many of their spoons were decorated with hammer marking that gave them a rather unfinished but hand-made look. The Guild of Handicraft, founded by Charles Robert Ashbee in 1888, was one of many organisations dedicated to the new style.

The movement was also strong in Scotland, particularly Glasgow, and designers such as Charles Rennie Mackintosh and many others at the Glasgow School of Arts produced drawings for items of flatware. Mackintosh's spoon designs tended, rather simply, to follow the trefid style of the later seventeenth century, although he produced some longer spoons with trefoil terminals for Miss Cranston's four lunch and tea rooms in Glasgow (the Sauchiehall Street rooms are still functioning). A few of these spoons were made in silver but most were electroplated and stamped with the mark MISS

Novelty spoon by the Guild of Handicraft to show 'the origin of the rat-tail', 1908.

Three spoons of antique derivation: the topmost of Romanesque style, produced at the Keswick School of Industrial Arts, 1929; a 1906 copy by H. Lambert of the famous St Nicholas spoon of 1528 (by John Carswell), probably made to commemorate the famous sale of the original in 1902, when it reached an unprecedented £690; a student piece (unmarked) of a classical style spoon with a seed pod finial and hammered finish, c.1900.

CRANSTONS, presumably to discourage theft! The present great interest in the works of Mackintosh has caused such spoons to be highly regarded by collectors and, as with Paul de Lamerie in the eighteenth century, the cachet of a leading name will multiply the value of even a humble item such as an electroplated teaspoon to a fantastic figure.

The Keswick School of Industrial Arts, founded in 1884 as a craft and metalworking school, among other institutes, produced spoons of a distinctly Romanesque style (look for the KSIA mark in an ellipse). Many other designers, including architects such as William Burges, tried

Part of a set of spoons designed by William Burges, c.1880, in the Romanesque-Gothic style. The spoons are part of a dessert service commissioned by the third Marquess of Bute for his secretary, George Edward Sneyd. The spoons were added as a personal gift from Burges and the donation inscriptions are recorded on the reverse of the bowls.

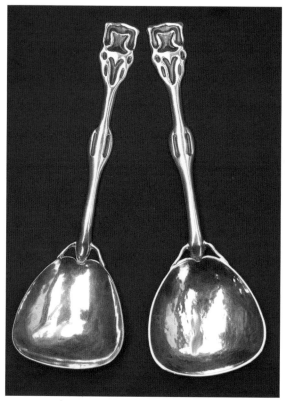

A pair of Art Nouveau enamelled spoons designed by Kate Harris and made by Hutton of Sheffield, assayed in London, 1903. One spoon has been left with a hammered finish while the other has been planished.

their hand at the designing of flatware. Burges's work included spoons that combined Romanesque with Gothic; examples are scarce, but some can be seen at the Victoria and Albert Museum.

As the style of French Art Nouveau and German Jugendstil evolved mainly from the Arts and Crafts movement at the start of the twentieth century, asymmetric swirls and curves, along with stylised natural motifs, crept into designs. English spoon bowls became more rounded or heart-shaped with a slight point to the front of the bowl, and handles were remarkably adorned in relevant taste, and sometimes colourfully enamelled. Equally amazing spoons, perhaps somewhat crudely made by art students, can

Two unmarked spoons of Art Nouveau (above) and Arts and Crafts (below) style. The upper spoon has been plique à jour enamelled within its interlacing handle, suggestive of Archibald Knox. The lack of marks and the slightly crude, hand-made look of these pieces suggest that they were made by qualifying students, c.1910 and c.1900.

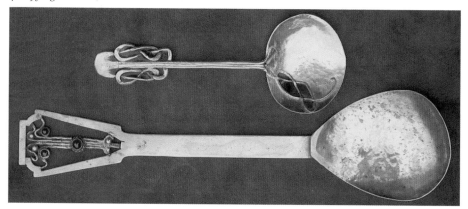

occasionally be found from this period. In London, the firm of Liberty used the talents of many designers, metalworkers and enamellers, some of whom were already well established and others of whom were just starting on their careers. They included Archibald Knox, Arthur Gaskin, Bernard Cuzner, A. E. Jones, Charles F. Varley and also the Birmingham firm of William Hair Haseler, the principal manufactory for Liberty's wares, including 'Cymric' (the Welsh name chosen by Liberty's head of production, John Llewellyn, perhaps patriotically, for the Liberty silverware). Silver spoons (mostly teaspoons) were included in the Cymric production line, some designed by Knox. Sets of half a dozen teaspoons were even made with diversely designed and enamelled handles. At first the company did not allow the artists to put their individual marks on these wares but, later, Haseler's WHH mark is often seen alongside the L&Co on a spoon handle or bowl back. In response to the success of the London-based Liberty, some of the Birmingham-based silversmithing firms, such as Nathan &

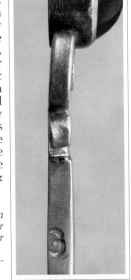

Below: *A fine Arts and Crafts spoon in medieval style, capped with a chrysoprase cabochon, by the husband and wife partnership of Arthur and Georgie Gaskin, 1902, inscribed 'Margaret Lindsay from her Godmother E.S.' on a glass dish by Sabino of Paris.*
Right: *The Gaskin incuse G mark on the handle of another (non-assayed) spoon.*

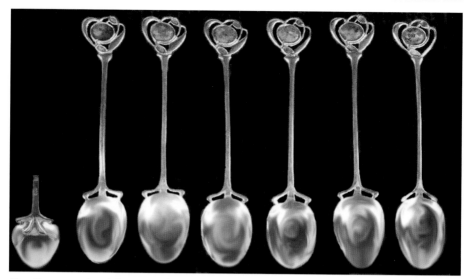

Six silver enamel-ended spoons, designed by Archibald Knox for Liberty & Co, 1904, typically combining Celtic with Art Nouveau; also showing the reverse of one spoon bowl.

A group of six Art Nouveau teaspoons relating to Liberty & Co: the three on the left are all of Birmingham assay, (from the top) 1906, 'Sarepta' 1902 (stamped Cymric) and 'Tree of Life' 1905, whose enamelled finial may be by C. F. Varley; (upper right) a fine example of the period by William Comyns, 1902; (middle right) by Nathan & Hayes, 1901; (lower right) a later and more Deco example by W. H. Haseler, also for Liberty, 1923, all on a Shelley Pottery plate, 'Physalis'.

Right: *The 'WHH' mark of Haseler's firm has been stamped over the 'L&Co' mark on this Liberty teaspoon, one of a set of six. Although the Liberty mark is intact on the other five spoons, this suggests that by 1910 Haseler was beginning to rebel against Liberty's ban on using his mark.*

Left: *A set of six enamelled rayed bowl teaspoons, typifying Art Deco style, in their original presentation box, by W. H. Haseler for Liberty, 1941.*

Hayes, began to produce extravagantly designed spoons as well.

Other European art movements included those of Josef Hoffmann and the Wiener Werkstätte (WW) in Austria, producing 'Secessionist' flatware, and the Württembergische Metalwaren Fabrik (WMF) in Germany. These were leaders in the style of the Viennese Secessionists, a breakaway group of artists who combined influence from Britain with their own ideas to produce an original style of Art Nouveau that spread to other European countries, notably Hungary. In the United States large silversmithing firms, Gorham especially, produced many original designs that typified American Arts and Crafts, and Louis Comfort Tiffany's firm produced items of more conformist flatware along with their other silver gifts.

In Britain the partnership of Omar Ramsden and Alwyn Carr produced many fine and highly collectable spoons that combined ancient and revived techniques of silversmithing. After their partnership was dissolved (1919), Ramsden continued to produce items in the traditional Arts and Crafts fashion through the 1920s and 1930s. Much of their work was signed, either in Latin (*Omar Ramsden me fecit* or *Ramsden et Carr me fecerunt*) or in English ('I was wrought by Omar Ramsden by command of ....'), although most spoons were too small for such flamboyance.

Charles Boyton designed and produced spoons and other flatware that conformed to the linearity and angular style of Art Décoratif, which superseded the swirls and curves of the Art Nouveau period. Some of Boyton's wares, known as Signature Cutlery, were stamped with his signature along the side of the handle so that it would not interfere with the design. Bernard Instone, who had been a student of Arthur

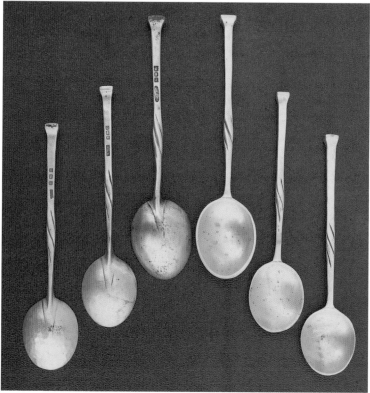

Six almost identical teaspoons, five by W. H. Haseler, 1933-8, and the sixth (top, back-facing) by Ramsden and Carr, 1917. The twisted stem and nail-head finial, characteristic of many of Ramsden's later spoons, may have been designed by Ramsden and Carr.

One of Ramsden's finest spoons, combining a triple-ended bowl support (after a seventh-century spoon from Barham Down) with Liberty-style Arts and Crafts splendour, made as late as 1934! In its original wooden box.

A pair of Art Deco spoons, 1937, by Charles Boyton, bearing his well-known signature, on a Paragon china plate, c.1930.

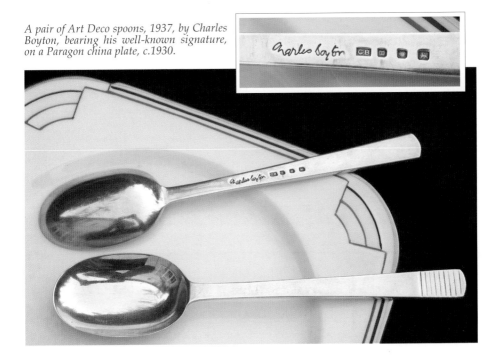

A large teaspoon with semi-oxidised copper button and filigree wire and with hammered finish, by Bernard Instone, 1902, and a set of Deco coffee spoons with colourful enamel handles, also by Instone, 1937, on a Grafton tea plate, c.1935.

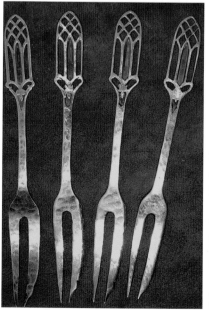

Gaskin, flourished as an enameller; his work is typified by his floral jewellery and he also produced some Art Deco flatware in the same style, and his spoons were often coloured with bright enamels. Earlier examples conformed more to Arts and Crafts taste with oxidised copper buttons and silver wire cabling on hammer-finished silver. Sibyl Dunlop, like Instone, produced colourful, if plainer, enamel-handled teaspoons and pastry forks, but in a mix of Arts and Crafts and Art Deco styles; her workshop manager, W. Nathanson, eventually persuaded her to progress into designs that were more in keeping with Deco taste.

In France the firm of Jean Puiforcat (born 1897) produced services and sets of table cutlery in varying designs, at first influenced by the Wiener Werkstätte but later developing his own styles, some of which

A set of pastry forks with interlacing arch finials and a hammered finish, by Sibyl Dunlop, 1927–8.

(Left to right) Two spoons and a fork from the renowned French firm of Jean Puiforcat; and a spoon, fork and knife embossed with fleurs-de-lys and with darkwood handles; a Danish spoon by Tøstrup and a dessert spoon by Tiffany, c.1890.

harked back to trefid flatware (a style that had originated in France). His flatware is always of the highest quality, hafted in varying materials, and has a strong following among the well-to-do. Wares that have acquired even the slightest age are highly collectable today.

Scandinavian designs continue to amaze, with flowing lines accentuated by minimalism (see the Tøstrup spoon, above). The Danish firms of Hertz and especially A. Michelsen produced spoons each Christmas, stamped with JUL (Yule) and

A group of Danish Christmas spoons and a Picasso-esque fork, 1950–80, mainly from A. Michelsen, but one by Hertz (1953).

Georg Jensen flatware, 'Kaktus' pattern, about 1930.

the year of production. These spoons now have something of a collector following, especially as they are appealingly colourful and each was carefully produced to delight. Another who produced Christmas wares was Georg Jensen (1866–1935), probably the best-known flatware and jewellery maker from Denmark. His designers produced patterns typical of their period. The best-known, 'Acorn' by Johan Rohde and 'Cactus' or *Kaktus* by Gundorph Albertus, exemplify the style of Jensen flatware; 'Art Deco' by Harald Nielsen, with its scoop-like fork (also found in other patterns) and handles styled with step and pommel finials, combines Secessionist with Deco. Jensen's earlier ventures in flatware included a rather important and frequently used cloud design by Thorvald Bindesbøll (c.1920). The design was used by several other Scandinavian flatware producers to decorate terminals and reflects a strong influence from Japanese metalwork. Jensen also produced miniature spoons using this design, and throughout the rest of Europe, particularly the Iberian countries, this tradition is continued to the present day.

PRESENT-DAY SPOONS

Among the commercial functionality of the plastic and disposable age, there are still a large number of craftspeople devoted to the designing and making of tableware, naturally

A scoop-like spoon in the form of a marrow, jocularly intended for marrow jam, complete with cucurbitaceous tendrils and leaves, by John Harry Fenn, 1983.

including spoons. Notwithstanding the strong influence from the Scandinavian countries, there are people who say that the designing and making of spoons has come full circle and that it is no longer possible to conceive new ideas without reference to the past. But spoons are versatile and essential items and, despite a long and broad design history, new styles continue to appear and to amaze – judging by the wares produced by such designers and goldsmiths as David Mellor, Stuart Devlin, Dennis Smith, Michael Bolton, Wally Gilbert and Harriet St Leger, to name but a few. Their wares can be viewed on the London Goldsmiths' Company website (www.thegoldsmiths.co.uk and www.whoswhoingoldandsilver.com). Another craftsman is John Harry Fenn, whose main craft is making dies from recycled rails, ploughs and other well-made steel. His designs are purely natural and unusually balanced, following an age-old tradition revived during the Arts and Crafts era. His spoons are carefully assembled from die-struck pieces of silver, in the form of leaves and tendrils, and are a delight to behold.

A fine-quality souvenir spoon of low-grade silver, but finely enamelled, depicting Port Said and with a Sphinx finial. It was probably purchased at the time when British interest in Egyptian antiquities was aroused by Howard Carter's discovery of Tutankhamun's tomb in 1922.

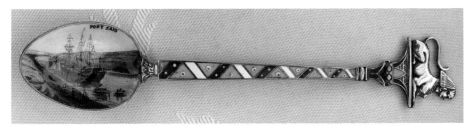

A highly individual and erotic set of spoons ornamented with gold and given individually to the author as Christmas and birthday presents between 2001 and 2004 by the London goldsmith Harriet St Leger.

The author is fortunate in having a partner who, following the Welsh tradition, hand-made a set of six silver love spoons with gold decoration over a three-year period – one for each Christmas and birthday. Harriet St Leger's set of spoons might have shocked shy, rural Welsh lovers of the eighteenth century, as they are explicitly erotic, but their sensual shape and overall design shows that each is a carefully designed and well-executed piece of art.

Further reading

Belden, G., and Snodin, M. *Spoons*. Walter Parrish International, 1976.

Caplan, N. 'Obsolete but charming – mote skimmers', *Country Life*, 175 (1984), pages 1704 and 1706.

Denn, G. 'Welsh love spoons', *Antique Dealer and Collectors' Guide*, 21 (1984), 42-3.

Eldred, E. 'Phineas Harris Levi, cometh the man – cometh the spoons', *The Finial* (Journal of the Silver Spoon Club of Great Britain), volume 15, number 4 (2005), pages 5 to 7.

Emery, J. *European Spoons before 1700*. John Donald, Edinburgh, 1976.

Gask, N. *Old Silver Spoons of England*. Herbert Jenkins, 1926.

Homer, R. F. *Five Centuries of Base Metal Spoons*. Published by the author and distributed by the Pewterers' Company, London, 1975.

Houart, V. *Antique Spoons – A Collector's Guide*. Souvenir Press, 1982.

Karlin, E. Z. *Jewelry and Metalwork in the Arts and Crafts Tradition*. Schiffer, Pennsylvania, 1993.

Kent, T. A. *Early West Country Spoons*. Exeter Museum, 1975. (The Corfield Collection.)

Kent, T. A. *London Silver Spoonmakers, 1500–1697*. The Silver Society, London, 1981.

Kent, T. A. *West Country Silver Spoons and Their Makers*. J. H. Bourdon-Smith, London, 1992.

Moore, S. J. *Cutlery for the Table (A History of British Table and Pocket Cutlery)*. Hallamshire Press, Sheffield, 1999.

Norie, J. *Caddy Spoons: An Illustrated Guide*. John Murray, 1989.

Pickford, I. *Silver Flatware*. Antique Collectors' Club, Woodbridge, Suffolk, 1983.

Price, F. G. H. *Old Base Metal Spoons*. Batsford, 1908.

Rainwater, D. T., and Felger, D. H. *A Collector's Guide to Spoons around the World*. Everybody's Press Inc, USA, 1976.

Riha, E., and Stern, W. B. 'Die römische Löffel aus Augst und Kaiseraugst', *Forschungen in Augst*, 5, 1982.

Snodin, M. *English Silver Spoons*. Charles Letts, 1974; revised edition, 1982.

Stevens, C. *Welsh Courting Customs*. Gomer Press, Ceredigion (UK), 1993.

Westman, O. *The Spoon*. Wiley & Putnam, London, 1845.

The Finial is a two-monthly illustrated bulletin produced by the Silver Spoon Club of Great Britain, 26 Burlington Arcade, Mayfair, London W1J 0PU. Telephone: 020 7491 1720. Website: www.bexfield.co.uk/thefinial   It contains articles and news and organises postal auctions of members' items.

Place setting of c.1770. The tea and dessert setting to the left. Note the bright-cut tablespoon on the famille rose plate (by Hester Bateman, 1778) and the bright-cut teaspoons with one feather-edged (left of threesome) by the Wedgwood cup. The two forks are (outer) a later Hanoverian of 1787 (top-marked), and a fiddle, thread and shell c.1770 alongside. The knives are typical of the period, with enamelled or green-stained ivory and silver capped hafts.

Places to visit

Many museums have a few spoons on display as part of their local heritage. The following are especially worthy of a visit. However, displays may be altered and readers are advised to telephone before visiting to check that relevant items are on show, as well as to find out opening times.

Allen Gallery, 10-12 Church Street, Alton, Hampshire GU34 2BW. Telephone: 01420 82802. Website: www.hants.gov.uk/museum/Allen The unique Elizabethan Tichborne spoons are displayed here.

Arlington Court (National Trust), Arlington, near Barnstaple, Devon EX31 4LP. Telephone: 01271 850296. Website: www.nationaltrust.org.uk Good collection of antique base-metal spoons.

Brecknock Museum, Captain's Walk, Brecon, Powys LD3 7DS. Telephone: 01874 624121. Website: http://powysmuseums.powys Love spoons.

The British Museum, Great Russell Street, London WC1B 3DG. Telephone: 020 7323 8000. Website: www.thebritishmuseum.ac.uk

Fitzwilliam Museum, Trumpington Street, Cambridge CB2 1RB. Telephone: 01223 332900. Website: www.fitzmuseum.cam.ac.uk

Holburne Museum of Art, Great Pulteney Street, Bath BA2 4DB. Telephone: 01225 466669. Website: www.bath.ac.uk/holburne

Museum of London, London Wall, London EC2Y 5HN. Telephone: 020 7600 3699. Website: www.museumoflondon.org.uk

Museum of Welsh Life, St Fagans, Cardiff CF5 6XB. Telephone: 029 2057 3500. Website: www.nmgw.ac.uk Love spoons.

Victoria and Albert Museum, Cromwell Road, South Kensington, London SW7 2RL. Telephone: 020 7942 2000. Website: www.vam.ac.uk

Weston Park Museum, Weston Park, Sheffield S10 2TP. Telephone: 0114 278 2600. Website: www.sheffieldgalleries.org.uk Good collection of early silver-plated flatware. (Formerly Sheffield City Museum; closed for redevelopment until spring 2006.)

Worshipful Company of Pewterers, Pewterers' Hall, Oat Lane, London EC2V 7DE. Telephone: 020 7606 9363. By appointment only. Website: www.pewterers.org.uk

Decorative salt spoon, inset with labradorite, in Arts and Crafts revival style by Helen West, 2000.

Index

These types of spoon are fast becoming prized by collectors. (Left to right) Teaspoon with pointed spade-shape bowl and with decorative finial, by A.E. Jones of Birmingham, 1905. Egyptian revival style teaspoon by V & S, Birmingham, 1930. Art Nouveau teaspoon designed by Kate Harris for Hutton of Sheffield and London, 1899. Magnificent Tudor-style spoon with frosted plique-à-jour enamelled frame terminal, c.1900, attributed to either the Gaskin or the Dawson partnerships. Three souvenir teaspoons – a Scottish thistle set with a faceted cairngorm (citrine) terminal by J. Grinsell & Sons, Birmingham, 1897; teaspoon with enamelled arms of Colwyn Bay by the famous partnership of Levi & Salaman, Birmingham, 1910; another by Levi & Salaman, Birmingham, with a terminal depicting an angel of peace (Pax) holding aloft an olive wreath, assayed in 1918 to commemorate the end of the First World War but issued in 1919.